MW01241739

DISCARD

our
Environment

Water Pollution

Peggy J. Parks

KIDHAVEN PRESS

An imprint of Thomson Gale, a part of The Thomson Corporation

THOMSON

★

™

GALE

Detroit • New York • San Francisco

LIBRARY OF CONGRESS CATALOGING-IN-PUBLICATION DATA

Parks, Peggy J., 1951–
    Water pollution / by Peggy J. Parks.
        p. cm.—(Our environment)
    Includes bibliographical references and index.
    ISBN-13: 978-0-7377-3667-0 (hardcover)
    1. Water—Pollution—Juvenile literature. I. Title.
    TD422.P37 2007
    363.739'4—dc22

                                                                    2007006893

ISBN-10: 0-7377-3667-4

Printed in the United States of America

contents

chapter one

Dirty Water

Water is essential for life. Not one living thing could survive without it. Almost three-fourths of Earth's surface is covered with water, and most is contained in the planet's vast oceans. Astronaut Edgar Mitchell once described this amazing view from high above the

A view of Earth from space.

planet: "Suddenly, from behind the rim of the moon . . . there emerges a sparkling blue and white jewel, a light, delicate sky-blue. . . . It takes more than a moment to fully realize this is Earth."[1] Other astronauts have made similar observations about the beauty of Earth from space. But there is a serious problem that is not visible from thousands of miles away: Much of the planet's water has been harmed by pollution.

Humans Versus Nature

Pollution occurs when harmful substances, or **pollutants**, build up in water and contaminate it. When small amounts of pollutants are present, water can get rid of them. It has the natural ability to clean itself through a process known as **weathering**. As soon as pollutants enter water, chemical and physical changes begin to take place. Wind, waves, and sunlight start breaking the pollutants down. Then they start to **biodegrade**, meaning bacteria and other natural **organisms** feed on them. Over time the pollutants will disappear.

Technicians test for groundwater pollution.

In many cases, however, humans release harmful substances into water faster than nature can break them down. Thus pollutants build up too fast for weathering to keep up. This results in water that is polluted and in some cases highly toxic. Pollution affects Earth's oceans, as well as lakes, rivers, streams, and wetlands. It also fouls **groundwater**, the vast supply of water found deep beneath Earth's surface. In the town of Ranipet, India, the groundwater has been severely polluted by toxic waste that has seeped into the ground from chemical factories.

Pollution Sources

Although there are many causes of water pollution, there are two basic types. One is **point source pollution**, which occurs when pollutants enter water directly through pipes or drains. Manufacturers of automobiles, chemicals, and electronics contribute to point source pollution, as do mining operations and paper mills. These and other in-

Paper mills contribute to point source pollution, releasing wastewater, known as effluents, into lakes, rivers, and streams.

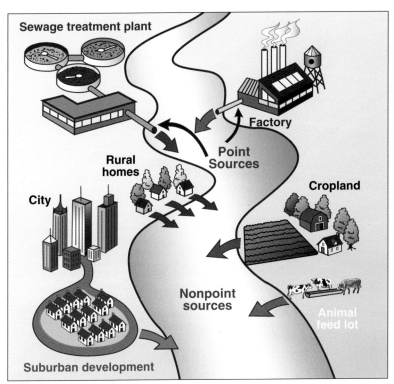

There are two basic types of water pollution: point sources and nonpoint sources.

dustries release wastewater, known as **effluents**, into lakes, rivers, and streams.

Nonpoint source pollution contaminates water in a different way. Rather than pollutants being discharged directly, they are washed into waterways during rainstorms. This is known as **runoff**. Oil, gas, and grease from vehicles contribute to runoff, as does salt that is used to melt snow and ice. These substances build up on roads and highways. Whenever it rains, they wash into storm sewers, or directly into streams, wetlands, lakes, and rivers. The pollutants can also seep into the groundwater below.

Mark Cousineau, president of a chapter of the environmental group Surfrider, points out a lagoon full of polluted runoff at Poche Beach in San Clemente, California.

Even careless household practices contribute to nonpoint source pollution. For instance, many people dispose of old paint, pesticides, and cleaning products by pouring them down the drain. When they change the oil in their vehicles, they may dump the used oil in drains or onto the ground. The pollutants eventually find their way into waterways, where they can cause serious environmental damage. For instance, just 1 gallon (3.8l) of used motor oil can pollute 1 million gallons (3.8 million l) of drinking water.

Oil and Water

Oil also pollutes water in many other ways, such as during accidental spills. When a ship sinks or runs aground, its oil tanks can rupture, sending oil pouring into the ocean. Major spills do not happen very often, but when they do, they can be devastating. The worst oil spill in the history of the Philippines occurred in August 2006 off the island of Guimaras. The tanker M/T *Solar 1* capsized in rough seas and sank, causing 132,000 gallons (500,000l) of oil to spill into the water. It formed a huge oil slick that began to spread rapidly. When it reached the shore, the sticky black goo coated hundreds of miles of coastline, including long stretches of white-sand, tropical beaches.

Oil does not always end up in the water by accident. Sometimes it is intentionally dumped, such as by crew members of ships. Vessels traveling through the oceans generate millions of gallons of a muddy waste product known as **oil sludge**. The National Academy of Sciences estimates that about 65 million

In 2006, the tanker M/T Solar 1 capsized in rough seas and sank, drenching the Guimaras Island coastline in oil.

gallons (247 million l) of the goopy sludge are released into the ocean each year. In 2004 a shipping company based in Hong Kong was prosecuted and fined millions of dollars for oil sludge pollution. Crew members of the MSC *Elena* were caught dumping the contaminated waste into the Atlantic Ocean. In just five months during 2004, the ship discharged nearly 11,000 gallons (42,000l) of oil sludge into the water.

Sewage
Ships also pollute Earth's water with sewage. Cruise ships, for instance, dump millions of gallons of raw sewage and wastewater directly into the

(Right) Black oil from a sunken tanker coats a penguin on Robben Island, off Cape Town, South Africa, June 26, 2000. (Bottom) A dog walks through crude oil spilled from a local refinery as a result of Hurricane Katrina, 2005.

Demonstrators protest waste dumping by the Star Princess cruise ship line in 2003. Cruise ships dump millions of gallons of raw sewage and wastewater directly into the ocean every year.

ocean every year. These massive vessels, often called floating cities, can legally dump the sewage as long as they are more than 3 miles (4.8km) from shore. But ships are only one source of sewage pollution. Cities and towns all over the world discharge sewage into nearby waterways. Much of it is treated before being released, but sometimes raw sewage is discharged. This is a problem in some parts of Canada. From the Saint Lawrence River to the Pacific Ocean, cities dump about 53 billion gallons (200 billion l) of raw sewage into waterways each year—enough to fill more than 40,000 Olympic-sized swimming pools. According to Canadian environmental officials, sewage is the country's leading source of water pollution.

Fertilizers and Pesticides

Another major source of water pollution is farming. Studies have shown that virtually every country that uses fertilizers and pesticides for agriculture has contaminated its water. This includes surface water as well as groundwater. Also, farm runoff is one of the biggest sources of pollution in the world's oceans.

A growing source of pollutants in America's waterways comes from concentrated animal feeding operations, or CAFOs. These enormous farms, which are often called factory farms, confine thousands of animals in one facility. The livestock produce massive amounts of animal waste—as much as 500 million

A helicopter sprays pesticides at a vineyard in Italy. Studies have shown that virtually every country that uses fertilizers and pesticides for agriculture has contaminated its water.

Concentrated Animal Feeding Operations, or CAFOs, confine thousands of animals in one facility and produce as much as 500 million tons (454 million metric tons) of animal waste per year.

tons (454 million metric tons) per year. The manure washes into rivers and streams during rainstorms. The Environmental Protection Agency (EPA) says that chicken, pig, and cattle waste from these CAFOs has polluted 35,000 miles (56,000km) of rivers, as well as the groundwater of seventeen states.

Chemicals in the Air

Just as water can be polluted by animal waste, oil, sewage, and other substances on the ground, pollution can also fall from the sky. Factories all over the world send toxic chemicals billowing into the atmosphere through their huge smokestacks. Vehicles traveling on the world's roads burn fuels that send toxic gases into the atmosphere through their tailpipes. Power stations burn coal, which emits sulfur dioxide and nitrogen dioxide into the air. Once these harmful

(Left) Toxic waste billows from smokestacks at a sugar plant in Clewiston, Florida. (Bottom) The toxic chemicals released from automobiles around the world contribute to the poor air quality in cities like Los Angeles and New York.

substances are in the air, they are blown around by winds and can travel hundreds of miles from their original source. They also mix with water vapor in the atmosphere. When it rains or snows, they fall to Earth and pollute water as well as land.

The world's water is being polluted in many ways. Industries contribute to pollution, as do vehicles, ships, agriculture, and people who use careless household practices in their homes. Even though water has the natural ability to clean itself, pollution often happens so fast that nature cannot keep up. Because of that, the world's most precious resource is in danger.

chapter two

Deadly Effects of Water Pollution

Water pollution occurs all over the world. But in the Russian city of Dzerzhinsk, the pollution is disastrous. The water is so contaminated that the *Guinness Book of World Records* lists Dzerzhinsk as the most polluted city in the world.

For many years chemical weapons were produced in Dzerzhinsk. During the manufacturing process, the factories improperly disposed of nearly 300,000 tons (272,000 metric tons) of chemical waste. This caused toxic chemicals to seep into the surface water and groundwater, turning it into a poisonous sludge. Environmental officials say that the chemical levels in the city's groundwater are extremely toxic—17 million times higher than what is considered safe. The water contains dioxins and phenol, which are some of the deadliest substances

The Guinness Book of World Records *lists the Russian city of Dzerzhinsk as the most polluted city in the world.*

in existence. Both can lead to liver damage, cancer, and other diseases. As a result of drinking the contaminated water, the people of Dzerzhinsk suffer from many types of health problems and rarely live past their mid-40s. According to Dr. Maradian, who works at a city hospital, the death rate is much higher than the rate of births: "If, on average, six to eight babies are born each 24 hours," he says, "15 to 18 people die. The situation is simply catastrophic."[2]

Toxic Buildup

Dzerzhinsk is a tragic example of what can happen when humans are exposed to seriously polluted water. By far, though, the greatest risk of water pollution is for babies and children. When children are very young, their brains, lungs, and nervous systems are not yet fully developed. Because the organs are so small, they are easily damaged by toxins. This is even true with children who have not been born. The Environmental Working Group (EWG) released a study of ten unborn children in July 2005. After performing tests, the EWG found that the fetuses' blood

This diagram shows the buildup of mercury in the food chain.

How mercury gets to your dinner table

Man-made pollution has increased the amount of mercury in the fish supply to sometimes harmful levels, especially for an unborn child.

First, coal-fired power plants release mercury into the atmosphere.

It can travel hundreds of miles before falling with the rain into lakes and streams.

Consumed by micro-organisms, mercury moves up the food chain and toward the ocean.

Fish at the top of the marine food chain accumulate levels of mercury that can do serious damage to the human nervous system when consumed regularly.

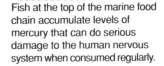

Large predatory fish	**Smaller saltwater fish**	**Shellfish**	**Freshwater fish**
At the top of the food chain, these fish acquire mercury levels above 1 part per million. The FDA recommends that pregnant women avoid swordfish, tilefish, king mackerel and shark altogether, or risk nervous system damage to an unborn child.	These fish such as cod and tuna can have levels between .17 and .60 ppm. The FDA recommends pregnant women not consume more than 12 ounces per week.	These can contain harmful levels of mercury with lobster leading the FDA list at .31 ppm.	Mercury levels vary according to the concentration in the water. Local officials should be contacted to assess mercury risk.

contained nearly 300 different toxic substances, including pesticides, dioxins, and mercury.

Of all the toxins that are known to exist, mercury is one of the most dangerous. Research has shown that the people who have the highest levels of mercury in their blood are those who eat large quantities of fish. The reason fish can be so toxic is because mercury builds up inside them. This is a process that happens over time and begins at the bottom of the **food chain**.

When mercury gets into lakes and rivers, it settles on the bottom and mixes with sediments. Microscopic organisms known as **zooplankton** live in the sediments, and they absorb the mercury. Tiny fish eat the zooplankton, and the mercury passes to them. Larger fish eat the smaller fish and absorb even higher levels of mercury. They are eaten by predators such as shark, tuna, dolphins, and swordfish. When people eat the fish, they also eat the mercury that was stored in the creatures' tissues.

Dangerous Sewage

Mercury and other toxic substances in water present serious risks for humans. But common household (or domestic) sewage is equally as hazardous. It contains harmful organisms known as **pathogens**. These organisms are too small to see without a microscope—but they are deadly. Pathogens can cause life-threatening diseases such as cholera, hepatitis, and typhoid. In undeveloped

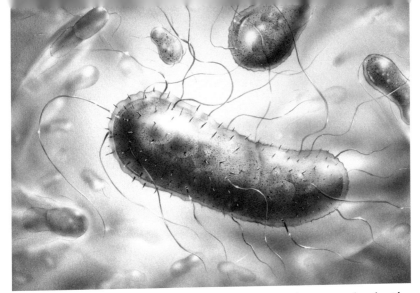

E. coli *bacteria, seen here in this illustration, can be both foodborne and waterborne. The O157:H7 strain can cause extreme sickness and even death in some cases.*

countries hundreds of thousands of people die every year from typhoid fever.

Diseases caused by pathogens claim lives in developed countries as well. In April 2006 a 34-year-old man named Oliver Johnson died after he was exposed to sewage pollution. Johnson lived in Honolulu, Hawaii. He fell into a harbor that had been contaminated with nearly 50 million gallons (189 million l) of raw sewage. Soon afterward he began to feel sick, but he waited a few days before going to the hospital. Doctors found that he had been infected by deadly flesh-eating bacteria. The infection began in his foot and then spread quickly through his bloodstream. Johnson developed severe blisters on his skin, and his body swelled up to three times its normal size. After the infection caused his kidneys and other vital organs to fail, he died.

Choked Waterways

Sewage pollution is also a serious threat to marine wildlife. That is because it can lead to **eutrophication**, or the premature aging of rivers and lakes. Sewage contains nutrients such as nitrogen and phosphorus. These substances build up in water and stimulate the growth of microscopic plants known

The process of eutrophication depletes the water of oxygen and blocks needed sunlight, causing fish and plant life to die.

Sunlight passes through water.

Plants produce oxygen that sea life needs to live.

Sunlight cannot pass through water.

Overgrowth of algae causes depletion of oxygen.

Sea life cannot live in water.

Hurricane Floyd created a brown "dead zone" of oxygen-depleted water near Cedar Island, North Carolina, in 1999.

as **phytoplankton**. This leads to massive growth in the zooplankton population, because the tiny creatures feed on phytoplankton. Seafloor bacteria thrive on the dead zooplankton and their waste and begin to multiply wildly. The result is a condition known as **hypoxia**, which occurs when oxygen in the water is choked out. Without oxygen, fish and other wildlife will eventually suffocate and die.

Another leading cause of eutrophication is agriculture. Runoff from farms contains animal waste, as well as chemical fertilizer and pesticides. Like sewage, when these substances wash into waterways, they stimulate plant growth. This has led to a serious problem in the Gulf of Mexico. Farmers along the Mississippi River use millions of tons of nitrogen fertilizer each year. It washes into the river during rainstorms and eventually ends up in the gulf. It has created a huge "dead zone" in the gulf where all aquatic wildlife has died. The zone covers an area of more than 5,000 square miles (13,000 sq. km)—

about the same size as the state of Connecticut. Marine biologist Nancy Rabalais scuba dives in the dead zone several times a month to keep track of changes. "You don't see any fish," she says, "[just decaying] bodies lying in sediment."[3]

Trash Takes Its Toll

Fish and other marine wildlife are also endangered because of trash pollution. Ocean cleanup operations have recovered everything from discarded truck tires to television sets, from toilets to infectious medical waste. By far one of the biggest threats to ocean creatures is plastic. According to the environmental group People & the Planet, more than 46,000 pieces of plastic litter are floating on every square mile of Earth's oceans. Of this litter, some of the most dangerous for wildlife are the plastic rings that hold beverage cans or bottles together. The rings can wrap around the creatures' necks and strangle them. Plastic bags and balloons are also threatening to wildlife. When dolphins, whales, seals, or other creatures see the items floating in the water, they can mistake them for food. If they eat the plastic, they can die from suffocation or intestinal blockage.

The Whale Rescue Team (WRT) works to save endangered wildlife in California. During 2004 the group rescued 165 marine mammals and more than 100 sea birds. One of the rescues involved a pregnant sea lion that was in danger of drowning. WRT volunteers could see that the creature was struggling

Volunteer whale rescue operation in Australia. Pollution in the form of plastics and other debris can also harm marine animals.

to stay upright on its flippers as it was battered by waves. When they reached the sea lion, they saw why it was having so much trouble: A plastic trash bag was wrapped around its body. "Marine animals suffer from many ailments that are out of our control to do something about," says Peter Wallerstein of the WRT. "The misery and death caused by trash that ends up along our coastline is something that we can and must eliminate."[4]

Tragic Effects

Water pollution occurs all over the world, from Dzerzhinsk, Russia, to the California coastline. It can be caused by sewage, trash, runoff from factory farms, or toxic waste. No matter where it happens or what causes it, the effects of pollution can be deadly —for the environment, for wildlife, and for humans.

chapter three

Water Pollution Crises

Li Yonggang has lived in China's Shanxi province his entire life. When he was a child, the nearby Sushui River was clear and clean and full of fish. Li has wonderful memories of growing up near the river and fishing with his friends. Today, however, the Sushui does not even resemble the river it used to be. Now it is one of China's most polluted bodies of water. The publication *China Daily* describes it as "black and smelly . . . more like a sewage ditch than a river."[5]

The Sushui is not the only river in Shanxi that has been spoiled by pollution. The other 25 rivers in the province are also badly polluted. In fact, the entire Shanxi region is more contaminated than any other place in China. Since the 1980s huge amounts of chemicals from dye factories and other industrial operations have been dumped into rivers, lakes, and streams. This pollution continues today. Factories in the Shanxi province generate about 3 million tons (2.7 million metric tons) of wastewater every day. About two-thirds of that waste is discharged directly into rivers. As Chinese industry continues its rapid growth in the coming years, environmental experts say that pollution in Shanxi is likely to grow even worse.

In 2005, chemical factory explosions poured 110 tons (100 metric tons) of benzene and other toxic chemicals into the Songhua River, which 9 millon people use for their drinking water.

China's Pollution Woes

Actually, China's water pollution crisis spreads far beyond the Shanxi province. The entire country has some of the most polluted water on Earth. In some rural areas, farmers who are too poor to buy bottled water take their water from contaminated wells. When it is boiled, a curdled scum forms on top. Wang Haiqing, a Chinese man who lives in the country near the town of Xiangcheng, explains: "It tastes metallic even after you boil it and skim the stuff off it. But it's the only water we have to drink and to use for cooking."[6]

One of China's worst water pollution problems is caused by sewage. Billions of tons of sewage are dumped into the country's rivers and lakes each year. In the Chinese province of Henan, tanneries, paper mills, and other industrial operations regularly dump

Pollution from a paper plant clogs the Yangtze River in China.

their waste into rivers. In the city of Chongqing, a stream called Qingshuixi is so polluted the water has turned black and smelly. Years ago it was called a pure stream because it was so sparkling clean. Now, however, it is highly contaminated by domestic and industrial waste. BBC News calls Qingshuixi a "bubbling, putrid pool of defecation and chemicals."[7]

China's longest river, the Yangtze, is severely polluted by fertilizer runoff from the many farms along its steep banks. The Yangtze is also badly polluted by waste from ships. Tens of thousands of vessels regularly travel through the river, and an estimated 90 percent of them dump their waste directly into the water. That amounts to more than 17 million tons (15 million metric tons) of sewage that ends up in the Yangtze every year. According to environmental officials, it is likely that pollution will cause it to become a "dead river" within five years.

In addition to pollution from intentional dumping, China's water is polluted by industrial spills. One such spill occurred in the fall of 2006 in the northern Chinese city of Lanzhou. In two separate accidents, wastewater from a heating plant gushed into the Yellow River and turned the water as red as blood. The previous year, an even more toxic spill happened in Jilin City, which is also in northern China. After a series of massive explosions at a chemical factory, 110 tons (100 metric tons) of benzene and other toxic chemicals spilled into the Songhua River. The contaminated water started flowing downriver with the current. When it wound its way through the city of Harbin, one of China's largest cities, the toxic slick was 50 miles (80km) long. It continued to move southward until it flowed into the Amur River and entered Russia. By the time the poisonous slick's journey ended, it had polluted the drinking water for millions of people. According to Chinese official Wen Jiabao, "The environmental situation is grim."[8]

Brazilian Disaster

Brazil has also suffered from toxic spills. One disastrous spill occurred in March 2003, at a pulp and paper manufacturing plant north of Rio de Janeiro. Like most paper producers, the Brazilian mill used extremely strong chemicals such as chlorine and sodium hydroxide (caustic soda) to bleach wood pulp. Its effluents were stored on the property in a massive storage tank. On March 29 the tank burst apart, causing more than 300 million gallons (1.2 billion l) of toxic wastewater to spill into the Paraíba do Sul and Pomba rivers. According to the World Wildlife Fund, the spill "was equivalent in size to losing half the water from a large dam."[9]

The chemicals in the effluents were extremely caustic—meaning they were strong enough to burn the skin off any living thing. As soon as the waste entered the rivers, it blackened the water and coated it with a thick layer of stinking foam. The foam began spreading fast, and as it moved along the surface, it killed everything in its path. In a very short time,

About 175 miles (280km) north of Rio de Janeiro, Brazil, caustic soda flooded the Pomba River due to a burst chemical reservoir on April 1, 2003.

thousands of dead fish were floating in the water. The chemicals killed hundreds of cattle and other livestock that drank water from the river, as well as all vegetation that grew on the river bottom or along the banks. Within days neither the Paraíba do Sul nor the Pomba had any sign of life whatsoever.

One area that was especially devastated by the Brazilian toxic waste spill was the fishing village of São Fidelis. For more than ten years, the town had een restocking the river with fish and freshwater lobsters. After the accident the people who made their living by fishing wondered how they would be able to survive. Joacy Ferreira Gonçalves, a leader of the São Fidelis fishing community, said his town used to be known as "the land of the freshwater lobster, but now it's the land of destruction."[10]

"The Water Is Full of Oil and Debris"

A different kind of spill occurred in July 2006 off the coast of Lebanon. During a military conflict between

Military conflict in Lebanon resulted in fuel storage tanks being hit by Israeli jets, causing the release of 17,000 tons (15,000 metric tons) of heavy fuel oil into the Mediterranean Sea.

Israel and militant fighters known as Hizballah, Israeli jets bombed a power plant near the city of Beirut. The jets targeted fuel storage tanks at the power plant—and when the tanks were hit, as much as 17,000 tons (15,000 metric tons) of heavy fuel oil gushed into the Mediterranean Sea. This created a massive oil slick nearly 100 miles (161km) long and more than 8 miles (13km) wide. It covered the entire coastline of Lebanon and spread to the neighboring country of Syria.

The oil spill has been called the worst environmental disaster in Lebanon's history. The gooey, thick, black oil coated countless fish and seabirds and washed the creatures ashore. It also damaged the area's ancient coral reefs. Zeina Alhajj, who studied the disaster for the environmental group Greenpeace International, describes the scene after the oil spill occurred: "All along the bay, it's just a strip of oil. The white sands have become black beaches. The water is full of oil and debris and dead fish. We saw crabs full of oil, struggling, fighting."[11] Environmental officials say damage from the oil spill is so severe that Lebanon may not recover from it for ten years.

In some countries of the world, the water is so badly polluted that it is considered a crisis situation. Whether the pollution is caused by years of intentional dumping or accidental spills, the result is great harm to the environment.

chapter Four

Saving Earth's Water

For many years, people have known that Earth's water is endangered because of pollution. In the United States, the severity of water pollution came to the public's attention in 1969. The Cuyahoga River in Cleveland, Ohio, caught fire—flames were actually shooting out of the water. No one was sure exactly how the fire started, but it was believed that sparks from a passing train ignited an oil slick on the river. An August 1, 1969, article in *Time* magazine described the fire and the condition of the Cuyahoga: "Some River! Chocolate-brown, oily, bubbling with subsurface gases, it oozes rather than flows. . . . The Federal Water Pollution Control Administration dryly notes: 'The lower Cuyahoga has no visible signs of life, not even low forms such as leeches and sludge worms that usually thrive on wastes.' It is also—literally—a fire hazard."[12]

Clean Water Legislation

The 1969 fire was not the first time the Cuyahoga River had erupted into flames. There had been nine other fires on the river since the late 1800s. But widespread publicity in magazines such as

The pollution-filled Cuyahoga River near Cleveland, Ohio, erupted into flames June 25, 1969.

Time, as well as newspaper stories and television coverage, helped increase the public's awareness of water pollution. Because of people's outrage over what happened in Cleveland, legislators began to work on laws that would protect the country's water. This led to the creation of the Federal Water Pollution Control Act of 1972. Commonly known as the Clean Water Act, it set strict limits on the substances that industries and sewage treatment plants could discharge into U.S. waterways. The legislation also provided $50 billion in funds for cities and states to build wastewater facilities.

The Freshwater Seas

Another important piece of legislation that was passed in 1972 was the Great Lakes Water Quality Agreement. The Great Lakes are so huge they are often called freshwater seas. Together, they contain one-fifth of the world's fresh surface water and nine-tenths of the freshwater in the United States. Before there were laws to protect them, they were threatened by sewage dumping, toxic effluents from industry, and agricultural runoff from farms.

Of the five Great Lakes, Lake Erie was in the worst shape. The shallowest and warmest of the Great Lakes, it had been polluted by industry and agriculture for many years. As Lake Erie's water became more polluted, algae and other vegetation grew and multiplied. This rapid growth choked out the lake's oxygen, which killed all the fish and other

A goldfish living in Lake Erie with saprolegnia *fungus, or "freshwater mold," near its tail. Water pollution is one of the contributing factors for the spread of* saprolegnia *in the Great Lakes.*

aquatic wildlife. By the 1960s the only life in the lake was the algae that covered the water's surface like a carpet of green moss. It was declared dead, as the Great Lakes Commission Web site explains: "Eutrophication had claimed Lake Erie and excessive algae became the dominant plant species, covering beaches in slimy moss and killing off native aquatic species by soaking up all of the oxygen."[13]

After the Great Lakes Water Quality Agreement was signed by the United States and Canada, Lake Erie and the other Great Lakes were protected from such serious pollution. There were also cleanup operations to remove existing pollutants. The lakes' protection was further strengthened in 1986 with the passage of the Great Lakes Toxic Substances Control Agreement.

Although these laws have not completely stopped water pollution in the Great Lakes, they have made a positive difference in the water quality.

A Global Problem

These sorts of laws help protect waterways in the United States, Canada, and other developed countries. But in some parts of the world, there is little or no regulation to help prevent water pollution. Factories are freely allowed to discharge their wastewater into rivers, lakes, and streams. This is the case in São Paulo, Brazil. Every day, tons of effluents from more than a thousand industries are dumped into the Tietê River. The river is severely polluted with toxic **heavy metals** such as lead, cadmium, and arsenic.

In China the lack of government regulation is a constant problem. That is a major reason why China suffers from such severely polluted lakes and rivers. Because of the desire to expand the Chinese economy, the government helps industries by passing only weak laws against industrial pollution. Even when laws do exist, government officials often do not enforce them.

Many countries also lack laws to prevent the dumping of raw sewage. This is most often the case in poor, developing nations that cannot afford good public sanitation systems. In India, for example, the city of Calcutta dumps 400 million tons (363 million metric tons) of raw sewage and other waste into coastal waters every year. About the same amount

Raw sewage flows untreated into the Ganges River in India, used by millions of devout Hindus every day.

of sewage is discharged into waterways in Mumbai, formerly Bombay, India. In the poverty-stricken town of Liluah, India, open sewers and drains have not been improved in 50 years. During the summer monsoon, a time of torrential rains and vast flooding, so much raw sewage floats down the streets of Liluah that cars cannot get through.

Safer Drinking Water

One of the biggest dangers of sewage and industrial waste pollution is the contamination of drinking water. In countries such as the United States, there are laws that regulate the quality of water from lakes, rivers, reservoirs, springs, and groundwater wells. All over the United States, cities have modern treatment plants that clean water and make it fit for people to drink. Chemicals such as chlorine are used to disinfect drinking water and make it safer.

Developing countries, however, usually cannot afford such treatment methods. As a result drinking water is often dangerously polluted. Many of these countries already have severe water shortages because their climates are very dry and they have such large populations. So, even though rivers, lakes, and streams in these regions are polluted, thirsty people have no choice but to drink water that can make them sick.

An organization called Water and Sanitation for the Urban Poor (WSUP) is working to help developing countries solve their water pollution problems. The group focuses on areas where the problems are most severe, such as India, Bangladesh, Brazil, and countries in Africa. WSUP works with local communities to help people understand the importance of keeping water clean. Another of the group's tasks is to help design and build water sanitation facilities. WSUP's goal is to assist 1 million people by 2008 and to increase that number to 4 million people by 2015.

Protection Against Oil Spills

Even where there are measures in place to protect water from pollution, there is always the risk of accidental spills. To help protect against oil spills, some countries have passed laws that tankers must obey. In the United States, Congress passed the Oil Pollution Act of 1990. It requires that all new oil tankers traveling through U.S. waters be built with double hulls. Older, single-hulled ships will only be allowed in U.S. waters until the year 2010. Other countries have also passed tougher laws for oil tankers, including France, Spain, and Australia. Ships that do not obey these laws risk being punished with huge fines. They may also be required to pay the cost of all cleanup operations if a spill occurs, which can amount to millions of dollars.

Water in the Future

As water pollution has continued to grow worse, people have become more aware of problems such as human disease, threats to wildlife, and the premature aging of lakes and rivers. Many countries have taken steps to prevent pollution and clean the water. The United States and other developed nations have passed laws that regulate everything from industrial discharge to the quality of drinking water. Even so, water throughout the world is still being polluted—and that means pollution is a serious global problem.

Notes

Chapter 1: Dirty Water

1. Quoted in Calvin J. Hamilton, "Earth from Space," Solar Views.com. www.solarviews.com/eng/earthsp.htm.

Chapter 2: Deadly Effects of Water Pollution

2. Quoted in Tim Samuels, "Russia's Deadly Factories," BBC News, March 7, 2003. http://news.bbc.co.uk/2/hi/programmes/correspondent/2821835.stm.
3. Quoted in Sierra Club, "The Dead Zone in the Gulf of Mexico." www.sierraclub.org/cleanwater/waterquality/deadzone.asp.
4. Peter Wallerstein, "Other Voices: Ocean Dumping Is Havoc for Marine Mammals," Friends of Animals, Spring 2005. www.friendsofanimals.org/actionline/spring-2005/other-voices.html.

Chapter 3: Water Pollution Crises

5. *China Daily*, "Rivers Run Black in Shanxi Province," July 17, 2006. www.china.org.cn/english/environment/174874.htm.
6. Quoted in Jim Yardley, "Rivers Run Black, and Chinese Die of Cancer," *New York Times*, September 12, 2004. www.wirednewyork.com/forum/showthread.php?t=5257.
7. Nick Mackie, "China's Murky Waters," BBC News, November 23, 2005. http://news.bbc.co.uk/2/hi/asia-pacific/4462574.stm.
8. Quoted in Geoff Dyer, Richard McGregor, and Neil Buckley, "Chinese Toxic Spill 'May Threaten Food Chain,'" *Financial Times*, November 24, 2005. www.

ft.com/cms/s/517d0e64-5d3a-11da-8cde-0000779e 2340.html.

9. World Wildlife Fund, "Toxic Disaster in Brazil," April 3, 2003. www.wwf.org.uk/News/n_0000000861. asp.

10. Quoted in Maria Osava, "Brazilian Chemical Spill Leaves 500,000 Without Water," *Asheville (NC) Global Report: Environment,* April 10–16, 2003. www.agrnews. org/ issues/221/environment.html#brazilian.

11. Quoted in Hannah Allam, "Huge Oil Spill off Lebanon Threatens to Ravage Life in the Sea," San Jose *Mercury News*, August 11, 2006. www.mercurynews.com/mld/ mercury news/news/world/15254329.htm.

Chapter 4: Saving Earth's Water

12. Quoted in Ohio History Central, "Cuyahoga River Fire." www.ohiohistorycentral.org/entry.php?rec=1642.

13. TEACH, "Water Pollution in the Great Lakes—Lake Erie: 'We Have Met the Enemy and He Is Us.'" www.great-lakes.net/teach/pollution/water/water5. html.

Glossary

biodegrade: To break down (or decompose) by natural means.

effluents: Liquids discharged as waste by industrial or sewage plants.

eutrophication: The aging process by which bodies of water are overly enriched by nutrients.

food chain: The transfer of food energy from organisms in one level to organisms in another level.

groundwater: Water supplies that exist deep beneath Earth's surface.

heavy metals: Metallic substances such as mercury, arsenic, lead, and cadmium that are highly toxic.

hypoxia: A lack of oxygen.

nonpoint source pollution: Pollution that occurs indirectly, such as through runoff.

oil sludge: Used motor oil.

organisms: Any living form of animal or plant life.

pathogens: Tiny organisms that can cause infection and disease.

phytoplankton: Microscopic plants that serve as food for zooplankton.

point source pollution: Pollution that occurs directly, such as when effluents or sewage are added to water through pipes.

pollutants: Any substances that cause harm to the environment.

runoff: Water that washes off the land during rainstorms.

weathering: The process by which pollutants undergo chemical and physical changes.

zooplankton: Microscopic animals that are eaten by fish.

For Further Exploration

Books

Nichol Bryan, *Exxon Valdez: Oil Spill*. Milwaukee: World Almanac Library, 2004. An informative story of the devastating 1989 oil spill in Alaska's Prince William Sound.

August Greeley, *Toxic Waste: Chemical Spills in Our World*. New York: PowerKids, 2003. Covers the many ways that chemicals are used today and explores the impact of spills on the environment, wildlife, and humans.

Rosie Harlow, *Garbage and Recycling*. New York: Kingfisher, 2001. Explains how many different kinds of waste can be recycled and includes tips for how young people can have a positive impact on the planet by recycling.

Periodicals

Kathryn Satterfield, "Coral Reef Rescue," *Time for Kids*, November 17, 2006.

Elizabeth Weise, "90 Percent of the Oceans' Edible Species May Be Gone by 2048, Study Finds," *USA Today*, November 2, 2006.

Web Sites

EcoKids (www.ecokids.ca). A site developed by Earth Day Canada that helps inform young people about environmental issues. Includes interactive games, animation, and a variety of fun activities.

Environmental Protection Agency Nonpoint Source Kids Page (www.epa.gov/nps/kids). Includes activities such as Darby Duck and the Aquatic Crusaders, puzzles, games, and links to other environmental sites designed for kids.

Oceanside Clean Water Program Kids Page (www. oceansidecleanwaterprogram.org/kids.asp). A site created by the city of Oceanside, California, that helps educate kids about water pollution.

Index

Picture credits

About the Author

Peggy J. Parks holds a bachelor of science degree from Aquinas College in Grand Rapids, Michigan, where she graduated magna cum laude. An avid fan of all things related to Earth science, astronomy, and the environment, Parks has written more than 50 books for Thomson Gale's KidHaven Press, Blackbirch Press, and Lucent Books imprints. She lives in Muskegon, Michigan, a town she says inspires her writing because of its location on the shores of Lake Michigan.